DOVER · THRIFT · EDITIONS

The Ballad of Reading Gaol and Other Poems

OSCAR WILDE

DOVER PUBLICATIONS, INC.
New York

DOVER THRIFT EDITIONS

EDITOR: STANLEY APPELBAUM

Published in Canada by General Publishing Company, Ltd., 30 Lesmill Road, Don Mills, Toronto, Ontario.

Published in the United Kingdom by Constable and Company, Ltd., 3 The Lanchesters, 162–164 Fulham Palace Road, London W6 9ER.

This Dover edition, first published in 1992, is a new selection of 24 works reprinted from a standard text, with a new Note and new alphabetical lists of titles and first lines. See the Note and the table of contents for further bibliographical data.

Manufactured in the United States of America
Dover Publications, Inc., 31 East 2nd Street, Mineola, N.Y. 11501

Library of Congress Cataloging-in-Publication Data

Wilde, Oscar, 1854–1900.
    The ballad of Reading Gaol and other poems / Oscar Wilde.
       p.   cm. — (Dover thrift editions)
   ISBN 0-486-27072-6 (pbk.)
   I. Title. II. Series.
PR5818.B2 1992
821'.8—dc20
                                                        91-29824
                                                             CIP

Note

OSCAR WILDE (born in Dublin, 1854; died in Paris, 1900) is equally famous for his plays, his short stories, his one novel and his poetry. The present volume is a new selection of 24 important poems, including the celebrated "Ballad of Reading Gaol," inspired by the author's two-year prison term in the 1890s.

This "Ballad" was originally published as a separate volume in 1898; similarly, the long poem "The Sphinx" had been published in a volume of its own in 1894. Sixteen of the other poems included here were first collected in the 1881 volume *Poems by Oscar Wilde*. The subsections into which that volume was divided are indicated in our table of contents, which also gives the years in which eight of these poems had been published individually for the very first time, in magazines. The last six poems included here were never collected in volumes in the poet's lifetime.

The poems written when Wilde was still in his early twenties, indicative of his precocious gifts, are already tinged with the thoughts of guilt and sin that were to beset him all his life. These and the later poems reveal debts to Shakespeare, Wordsworth, Poe, Swinburne and folk balladry, and are distinguished by archaic or arcane vocabulary, Oriental eroticism, a preoccupation with prostitutes and a concern with the visual arts, especially the art of Whistler. "The Ballad of Reading Gaol" is outstanding for its sincerity, reflected in its simpler language and New Testament references. The posthumously published "To L. L." is perhaps the most refreshingly natural and human utterance of all.

Contents

Dates in square brackets following titles of individual poems are those of first publications in periodicals.

The Ballad of Reading Gaol
and Other Poems

Hélas ! *

To drift with every passion till my soul
Is a stringed lute on which all winds can play,
Is it for this that I have given away
Mine ancient wisdom, and austere control?
Methinks my life is a twice-written scroll
Scrawled over on some boyish holiday
With idle songs for pipe and virelay,
Which do but mar the secret of the whole.
Surely there was a time I might have trod
The sunlit heights, and from life's dissonance
Struck one clear chord to reach the ears of God:
Is that time dead? lo! with a little rod
I did but touch the honey of romance—
And must I lose a soul's inheritance?

* Alas.

To Milton

Milton! I think thy spirit hath passed away
From these white cliffs and high-embattled towers;
    This gorgeous fiery-coloured world of ours
Seems fallen into ashes dull and grey,
And the age changed unto a mimic play
    Wherein we waste our else too-crowded hours:
    For all our pomp and pageantry and powers
We are but fit to delve the common clay,
Seeing this little isle on which we stand,
    This England, this sea-lion of the sea,
    By ignorant demagogues is held in fee,
Who love her not: Dear God! is this the land
    Which bare a triple empire in her hand
    When Cromwell spake the word Democracy!

Requiescat

Tread lightly, she is near
  Under the snow,
Speak gently, she can hear
  The daisies grow.

All her bright golden hair
  Tarnished with rust,
She that was young and fair
  Fallen to dust.

Lily-like, white as snow,
  She hardly knew
She was a woman, so
  Sweetly she grew.

Coffin-board, heavy stone,
  Lie on her breast,
I vex my heart alone,
  She is at rest.

Peace, peace, she cannot hear
  Lyre or sonnet,
All my life's buried here,
  Heap earth upon it.

Avignon

Vita Nuova

I stood by the unvintageable sea
  Till the wet waves drenched face and hair with spray ;
  The long red fires of the dying day
Burned in the west ; the wind piped drearily ;
And to the land the clamorous gulls did flee :
  " Alas ! " I cried, " my life is full of pain,
  And who can garner fruit or golden grain
From these waste fields which travel ceaselessly ! "
My nets gaped wide with many a break and flaw,
  Nathless I threw them as my final cast

Into the sea, and waited for the end.
When lo ! a sudden glory ! and I saw
   The argent splendour of white limbs ascend,
And in that joy forgot my tortured past.

Impression du Matin

The Thames nocturne of blue and gold
   Changed to a Harmony in grey :
   A barge with ochre-coloured hay
Dropt from the wharf : and chill and cold

The yellow fog came creeping down
   The bridges, till the houses' walls
   Seemed changed to shadows and St. Paul's
Loomed like a bubble o'er the town.

Then suddenly arose the clang
   Of waking life ; the streets were stirred
   With country waggons : and a bird
Flew to the glistening roofs and sang.

But one pale woman all alone,
   The daylight kissing her wan hair,
   Loitered beneath the gas lamps' flare,
With lips of flame and heart of stone.

Chanson

A ring of gold and a milk-white dove
   Are goodly gifts for thee,
And a hempen rope for your own love
   To hang upon a tree.

For you a House of Ivory,
   (Roses are white in the rose-bower) !
A narrow bed for me to lie,
   (White, O white, is the hemlock flower) !

Myrtle and jessamine for you
   (O the red rose is fair to see) !
For me the cypress and the rue,
   (Finest of all is rosemary) !

For you three lovers of your hand,
   (Green grass where a man lies dead) !
For me three paces on the sand,
   (Plant lilies at my head) !

Impressions

I

Les Silhouettes

The sea is flecked with bars of grey,
The dull dead wind is out of tune,
And like a withered leaf the moon
Is blown across the stormy bay.

Etched clear upon the pallid sand
The black boat lies : a sailor boy
Clambers aboard in careless joy
With laughing face and gleaming hand.

And overhead the curlews cry,
Where through the dusky upland grass
The young brown-throated reapers pass,
Like silhouettes against the sky.

2

La Fuite de la Lune *

To outer senses there is peace,
A dreamy peace on either hand,
Deep silence in the shadowy land,
Deep silence where the shadows cease.

* The Flight of the Moon.

Save for a cry that echoes shrill
From some lone bird disconsolate ;
A corncrake calling to its mate ;
The answer from the misty hill.

And suddenly the moon withdraws
Her sickle from the lightening skies,
And to her sombre cavern flies,
Wrapped in a veil of yellow gauze.

The Grave of Keats

Rid of the world's injustice, and his pain,
He rests at last beneath God's veil of blue.
Taken from life when life and love were new
The youngest of the martyrs here is lain,
    Fair as Sebastian, and as early slain.
    No cypress shades his grave, no funeral yew,
    But gentle violets weeping with the dew
Weave on his bones an ever-blossoming chain.
O proudest heart that broke for misery !
    O sweetest lips since those of Mitylene !
    O poet-painter of our English Land !
Thy name was writ in water—it shall stand :
    And tears like mine will keep thy memory green,
As Isabella did her Basil-tree.

ROME

Ballade de Marguerite

(Normande)

I am weary of lying within the chase
When the knights are meeting in market-place.

Nay, go not thou to the red-roofed town
Lest the hooves of the war-horse tread thee down.

But I would not go where the Squires ride,
I would only walk by my Lady's side.

Alack ! and alack ! thou art overbold,
A Forester's son may not eat off gold.

Will she love me the less that my Father is seen
Each Martinmas day in a doublet green ?

Perchance she is sewing at tapestrie,
Spindle and loom are not meet for thee.

Ah, if she is working the arras bright
I might ravel the threads by the fire-light.

Perchance she is hunting of the deer,
How could you follow o'er hill and mere ?

Ah, if she is riding with the court,
I might run beside her and wind the morte.

Perchance she is kneeling in St. Denys,
(On her soul may our Lady have gramercy !)

Ah, if she is praying in lone chapelle,
I might swing the censer and ring the bell.

Come in, my son, for you look sae pale,
The father shall fill thee a stoup of ale.

But who are these knights in bright array ?
Is it a pageant the rich folks play ?

'Tis the King of England from over sea,
Who has come unto visit our fair countrie.

But why does the curfew toll sae low ?
And why do the mourners walk a-row ?

O 't is Hugh of Amiens my sister's son
Who is lying stark, for his day is done.

Nay, nay, for I see white lilies clear,
It is no strong man who lies on the bier.

O 't is old Dame Jeannette that kept the hall,
I knew she would die at the autumn fall.

Dame Jeannette had not that gold-brown hair,
Old Jeannette was not a maiden fair.

O 't is none of our kith and none of our kin,
(Her soul may our Lady assoil from sin !)

But I hear the boy's voice chaunting sweet,
" Elle est morte, la Marguerite."

Come in, my son, and lie on the bed,
And let the dead folk bury their dead.

O mother, you know I loved her true :
O mother, hath one grave room for two ?

Impression de Voyage

The sea was sapphire coloured, and the sky
  Burned like a heated opal through the air ;
  We hoisted sail ; the wind was blowing fair
For the blue lands that to the eastward lie.
From the steep prow I marked with quickening eye
  Zakynthos, every olive grove and creek,
  Ithaca's cliff, Lycaon's snowy peak,
And all the flower-strewn hills of Arcady.
The flapping of the sail against the mast,
  The ripple of the water on the side,
  The ripple of girls' laughter at the stern,
The only sounds :—when 'gan the West to burn,
  And a red sun upon the seas to ride.
  I stood upon the soil of Greece at last !

Panthea

Nay, let us walk from fire unto fire,
  From passionate pain to deadlier delight,—
I am too young to live without desire,
  Too young art thou to waste this summer night
Asking those idle questions which of old
Man sought of seer and oracle, and no reply was told.

For, sweet, to feel is better than to know,
    And wisdom is a childless heritage,
One pulse of passion—youth's first fiery glow,—
    Are worth the hoarded proverbs of the sage :
Vex not thy soul with dead philosophy,
Have we not lips to kiss with, hearts to love and eyes to see !

Dost thou not hear the murmuring nightingale,
    Like water bubbling from a silver jar,
So soft she sings the envious moon is pale,
    That high in heaven she is hung so far
She cannot hear that love-enraptured tune,—
Mark how she wreathes each horn with mist, yon late and
    labouring moon.

White lilies, in whose cups the gold bees dream,
    The fallen snow of petals where the breeze
Scatters the chestnut blossom, or the gleam
    Of boyish limbs in water,—are not these
Enough for thee, dost thou desire more ?
Alas ! the Gods will give nought else from their eternal store.

For our high Gods have sick and wearied grown
    Of all our endless sins, our vain endeavour
For wasted days of youth to make atone
    By pain or prayer or priest, and never, never,
Hearken they now to either good or ill,
But send their rain upon the just and the unjust at will.

They sit at ease, our Gods they sit at ease,
    Strewing with leaves of rose their scented wine,
They sleep, they sleep, beneath the rocking trees
    Where asphodel and yellow lotus twine,
Mourning the old glad days before they knew
What evil things the heart of man could dream, and dreaming
    do.

And far beneath the brazen floor they see
    Like swarming flies the crowd of little men,
The bustle of small lives, then wearily
    Back to their lotus-haunts they turn again
Kissing each others' mouths, and mix more deep
The poppy-seeded draught which brings soft purple-lidded
    sleep.

There all day long the golden-vestured sun,
　　Their torch-bearer, stands with his torch ablaze,
And, when the gaudy web of noon is spun
　　By its twelve maidens, through the crimson haze
Fresh from Endymion's arms comes forth the moon,
And the immortal Gods in toils of mortal passions swoon.

There walks Queen Juno through some dewy mead,
　　Her grand white feet flecked with the saffron dust
Of wind-stirred lilies, while young Ganymede
　　Leaps in the hot and amber-foaming must,
His curls all tossed, as when the eagle bare
The frightened boy from Ida through the blue Ionian air.

There in the green heart of some garden close
　　Queen Venus with the shepherd at her side,
Her warm soft body like the briar rose
　　Which would be white yet blushes at its pride,
Laughs low for love, till jealous Salmacis
Peers through the myrtle-leaves and sighs for pain of lonely bliss.

There never does that dreary north-wind blow
　　Which leaves our English forests bleak and bare,
Nor ever falls the swift white-feathered snow,
　　Nor ever doth the red-toothed lightning dare
To wake them in the silver-fretted night
When we lie weeping for some sweet sad sin, some dead delight.

Alas ! they know the far Lethæan spring,
　　The violet-hidden waters well they know,
Where one whose feet with tired wandering
　　Are faint and broken may take heart and go,
And from those dark depths cool and crystalline
Drink, and draw balm, and sleep for sleepless souls, and ano-
　　dyne.

But we oppress our natures, God or Fate
　　Is our enemy, we starve and feed
On vain repentance—O we are born too late !
　　What balm for us in bruisèd poppy seed
Who crowd into one finite pulse of time
The joy of infinite love and the fierce pain of infinite crime.

O we are wearied of this sense of guilt,
　　Wearied of pleasure's paramour despair,

Wearied of every temple we have built,
  Wearied of every right, unanswered prayer,
For man is weak ; God sleeps ; and heaven is high ;
One fiery-coloured moment : one great love ; and lo ! we die.

Ah ! but no ferry-man with labouring pole
  Nears his black shallop to the flowerless strand,
No little coin of bronze can bring the soul
  Over Death's river to the sunless land,
Victim and wine and vow are all in vain,
The tomb is sealed ; the soldiers watch ; the dead rise not again.

We are resolved into the supreme air,
  We are made one with what we touch and see,
With our heart's blood each crimson sun is fair,
  With our young lives each spring-impassioned tree
Flames into green, the wildest beasts that range
The moor our kinsmen are, all life is one, and all is change.

With beat of systole and of diastole
  One grand great life throbs through earth's giant heart,
And mighty waves of single Being roll
  From nerveless germ to man, for we are part
Of every rock and bird and beast and hill,
One with the things that prey on us, and one with what we kill.

From lower cells of waking life we pass
  To full perfection ; thus the world grows old :
We who are godlike now were once a mass
  Of quivering purple flecked with bars of gold,
Unsentient or of joy or misery,
And tossed in terrible tangles of some wild and wind-swept sea.

This hot hard flame with which our bodies burn
  Will make some meadow blaze with daffodil,
Ay ! and those argent breasts of thine will turn
  To water-lilies ; the brown fields men till
Will be more fruitful for our love to-night,
Nothing is lost in nature, all things live in Death's despite.

The boy's first kiss, the hyacinth's first bell,
  The man's last passion, and the last red spear
That from the lily leaps, the asphodel
  Which will not let its blossoms blow for fear
Of too much beauty, and the timid shame

Of the young bridegroom at his lover's eyes,—these with the
    same

One sacrament are consecrate, the earth
    Not we alone hath passions hymeneal,
The yellow buttercups that shake for mirth
    At daybreak know a pleasure not less real
Than we do, when in some fresh-blossoming wood,
We draw the spring into our hearts, and feel that life is good.

So when men bury us beneath the yew
    Thy crimson-stainèd mouth a rose will be,
And thy soft eyes lush bluebells dimmed with dew,
    And when the white narcissus wantonly
Kisses the wind its playmate some faint joy
Will thrill our dust, and we will be again fond maid and boy.

And thus without life's conscious torturing pain
    In some sweet flower we will feel the sun,
And from the linnet's throat will sing again,
    And as two gorgeous-mailèd snakes will run
Over our graves, or as two tigers creep
Through the hot jungle where the yellow-eyed huge lions sleep

And give them battle ! How my heart leaps up
    To think of that grand living after death
In beast and bird and flower, when this cup,
    Being filled too full of spirit, bursts for breath,
And with the pale leaves of some autumn day
The soul earth's earliest conqueror becomes earth's last great
    prey.

O think of it ! We shall inform ourselves
    Into all sensuous life, the goat-foot Faun,
The Centaur, or the merry bright-eyed Elves
    That leave their dancing rings to spite the dawn
Upon the meadows, shall not be more near
Than you and I to nature's mysteries, for we shall hear

The thrush's heart beat, and the daisies grow,
    And the wan snowdrop sighing for the sun
On sunless days in winter, we shall know
    By whom the silver gossamer is spun,
Who paints the diapered fritillaries,
On what wide wings from shivering pine to pine the eagle flies.

Ay ! had we never loved at all, who knows
   If yonder daffodil had lured the bee
Into its gilded womb, or any rose
   Had hung with crimson lamps its little tree !
Methinks no leaf would ever bud in spring,
But for the lovers' lips that kiss, the poets' lips that sing.

Is the light vanished from our golden sun,
   Or is this dædal-fashioned earth less fair,
That we are nature's heritors, and one
   With every pulse of life that beats the air ?
Rather new suns across the sky shall pass,
New splendour come unto the flower, new glory to the grass.

And we two lovers shall not sit afar,
   Critics of nature, but the joyous sea
Shall be our raiment, and the bearded star
   Shoot arrows at our pleasure ! We shall be
Part of the mighty universal whole,
And through all æons mix and mingle with the Kosmic Soul !

We shall be notes in that great Symphony
   Whose cadence circles through the rhythmic spheres,
And all the live World's throbbing heart shall be
   One with our heart ; the stealthy creeping years
Have lost their terrors now, we shall not die,
The Universe itself shall be our Immortality.

Impression

Le Réveillon

The sky is laced with fitful red,
   The circling mists and shadows flee,
   The dawn is rising from the sea,
Like a white lady from her bed.

And jagged brazen arrows fall
   Athwart the feathers of the night,
   And a long wave of yellow light
Breaks silently on tower and hall,

And spreading wide across the wold,
    Wakes into flight some fluttering bird,
And all the chestnut tops are stirred,
    And all the branches streaked with gold.

Apologia

Is it thy will that I should wax and wane,
    Barter my cloth of gold for hodden grey,
And at thy pleasure weave that web of pain
    Whose brightest threads are each a wasted day ?

Is it thy will—Love that I love so well—
    That my Soul's House should be a tortured spot
Wherein, like evil paramours, must dwell
    The quenchless flame, the worm that dieth not ?

Nay, if it be thy will I shall endure,
    And sell ambition at the common mart,
And let dull failure be my vestiture,
    And sorrow dig its grave within my heart.

Perchance it may be better so—at least
    I have not made my heart a heart of stone,
Nor starved my boyhood of its goodly feast,
    Nor walked where Beauty is a thing unknown.

Many a man hath done so ; sought to fence
    In straitened bonds the soul that should be free,
Trodden the dusty road of common sense,
    While all the forest sang of liberty,

Not marking how the spotted hawk in flight
    Passed on wide pinion through the lofty air,
To where some steep untrodden mountain height
    Caught the last tresses of the Sun God's hair.

Or how the little flower be trod upon,
    The daisy, that white-feathered shield of gold,
Followed with wistful eyes the wandering sun
    Content if once its leaves were aureoled.

But surely it is something to have been
　　The best belovèd for a little while,
To have walked hand in hand with Love, and seen
　　His purple wings flit once across thy smile.

Ay ! though the gorgèd asp of passion feed
　　On my boy's heart, yet have I burst the bars,
Stood face to face with Beauty, known indeed
　　The Love which moves the Sun and all the stars !

Silentium Amoris *

As often-times the too resplendent sun
　　Hurries the pallid and reluctant moon
Back to her sombre cave, ere she hath won
　　A single ballad from the nightingale,
　　So doth thy Beauty make my lips to fail,
And all my sweetest singing out of tune.

And as at dawn across the level mead
　　On wings impetuous some wind will come,
And with its too harsh kisses break the reed
　　Which was its only instrument of song,
　　So my too stormy passions work me wrong,
And for excess of Love my Love is dumb.

But surely unto Thee mine eyes did show
　　Why I am silent, and my lute unstrung ;
Else it were better we should part, and go,
　　Thou to some lips of sweeter melody,
　　And I to nurse the barren memory
Of unkissed kisses, and songs never sung.

* The Silence of Love.

Tædium Vitæ *

To stab my youth with desperate knives, to wear
This paltry age's gaudy livery,
To let each base hand filch my treasury,
To mesh my soul within a woman's hair,
And be mere Fortune's lackeyed groom,—I swear
I love it not ! these things are less to me
Than the thin foam that frets upon the sea,
Less than the thistledown of summer air
Which hath no seed : better to stand aloof
Far from these slanderous fools who mock my life
Knowing me not, better the lowliest roof
Fit for the meanest hind to sojourn in,
Than to go back to that hoarse cave of strife
Where my white soul first kissed the mouth of sin.

* Weariness of Life.

ΓΛΥΚΥΠΙΚΡΟΣ ΕΡΩΣ

Sweet, I blame you not, for mine the fault was, had I
    not been made of common clay
I had climbed the higher heights unclimbed yet, seen
    the fuller air, the larger day.

From the wildness of my wasted passion I had struck a
    better, clearer song,
Lit some lighter light of freer freedom, battled with
    some Hydra-headed wrong.

Had my lips been smitten into music by the kisses that
    but made them bleed,
You had walked with Bice and the angels on that ver-
    dant and enamelled mead.

I had trod the road which Dante treading saw the suns
    of seven circles shine,
Ay ! perchance had seen the heavens opening, as they
    opened to the Florentine.

And the mighty nations would have crowned me, who
    am crownless now and without name,

And some orient dawn had found me kneeling on the
    threshold of the House of Fame.

I had sat within that marble circle where the oldest bard
    is as the young,
And the pipe is ever dropping honey, and the lyre's
    strings are ever strung.

Keats had lifted up his hymeneal curls from out the
    poppy-seeded wine,
With ambrosial mouth had kissed my forehead,
    clasped the hand of noble love in mine.

And at springtide, when the apple-blossoms brush the
    burnished bosom of the dove,
Two young lovers lying in an orchard would have read
    the story of our love.

Would have read the legend of my passion, known the
    bitter secret of my heart,
Kissed as we have kissed, but never parted as we two are
    fated now to part.

For the crimson flower of our life is eaten by the canker-
    worm of truth
And no hand can gather up the fallen petals of the
    withered rose of youth.

Yet I am not sorry that I loved you—ah ! what else had I
    a boy to do,—
For the hungry teeth of time devour, and the silent-
    footed years pursue.

Rudderless, we drift athwart a tempest, and when once
    the storm of youth is past,
Without lyre, without lute or chorus, Death the silent
    pilot comes at last.

And within the grave there is no pleasure, for the blind-
    worm battens on the root,
And Desire shudders into ashes, and the tree of Passion
    bears no fruit.

Ah ! what else had I to do but love you, God's own
    mother was less dear to me,
And less dear the Cytheræan rising like an argent lily
    from the sea.

I have made my choice, have lived my poems, and,
    though youth is gone in wasted days,
I have found the lover's crown of myrtle better than the
    poet's crown of bays.

The Sphinx

In a dim corner of my room for longer than my fancy
    thinks
A beautiful and silent Sphinx has watched me through
    the shifting gloom.

Inviolate and immobile she does not rise she does not
    stir
For silver moons are naught to her and naught to her
    the suns that reel.

Red follows grey across the air, the waves of moonlight
    ebb and flow
But with the Dawn she does not go and in the night-
    time she is there.

Dawn follows Dawn and Nights grow old and all the
    while this curious cat
Lies couching on the Chinese mat with eyes of satin
    rimmed with gold.

Upon the mat she lies and leers and on the tawny throat
    of her
Flutters the soft and silky fur or ripples to her pointed
    ears.

Come forth, my lovely seneschal! so somnolent, so
    statuesque!
Come forth you exquisite grotesque! half woman and
    half animal!

Come forth my lovely languorous Sphinx! and put
    your head upon my knee!
And let me stroke your throat and see your body spotted
    like the Lynx!

And let me touch those curving claws of yellow ivory
    and grasp

The tail that like a monstrous Asp coils round your
    heavy velvet paws !

A thousand weary centuries are thine while I have
    hardly seen
Some twenty summers cast their green for Autumn's
    gaudy liveries.

But you can read the Hieroglyphs on the great sand-
    stone obelisks,
And you have talked with Basilisks, and you have
    looked on Hippogriffs.

O tell me, were you standing by when Isis to Osiris
    knelt ?
And did you watch the Egyptian melt her union for
    Antony

And drink the jewel-drunken wine and bend her head
    in mimic awe
To see the huge proconsul draw the salted tunny from
    the brine ?

And did you mark the Cyprian kiss white Adon on his
    catafalque ?
And did you follow Amenalk, the God of Heliopolis ?

And did you talk with Thoth, and did you hear the
    moon-horned Io weep ?
And know the painted kings who sleep beneath the
    wedge-shaped Pyramid ?

Lift up your large black satin eyes which are like cush-
    ions where one sinks !
Fawn at my feet, fantastic Sphinx ! and sing me all your
    memories !

Sing to me of the Jewish maid who wandered with the
    Holy Child,
And how you led them through the wild, and how they
    slept beneath your shade.

Sing to me of that odorous green eve when crouching
    by the marge
You heard from Adrian's gilded barge the laughter of
    Antinous

And lapped the stream and fed your drouth and
    watched with hot and hungry stare

The ivory body of that rare young slave with his pome-
granate mouth !

Sing to me of the Labyrinth in which the two-formed
bull was stalled !
Sing to me of the night you crawled across the temple's
granite plinth

When through the purple corridors the screaming scar-
let Ibis flew
In terror, and a horrid dew dripped from the moaning
Mandragores,

And the great torpid crocodile within the tank shed
slimy tears,
And tare the jewels from his ears and staggered back
into the Nile,

And the priests cursed you with shrill psalms as in your
claws you seized their snake
And crept away with it to slake your passion by the
shuddering palms.

Who were your lovers ? who were they who wrestled for
you in the dust ?
Which was the vessel of your Lust ? What Leman had
you, every day ?

Did giant Lizards come and crouch before you on the
reedy banks ?
Did Gryphons with great metal flanks leap on you in
your trampled couch ?

Did monstrous hippopotami come sidling toward you
in the mist ?
Did gilt-scaled dragons writhe and twist with passion as
you passed them by ?

And from the brick-built Lycian tomb what horrible
Chimera came
With fearful heads and fearful flame to breed new
wonders from your womb ?

Or had you shameful secret quests and did you harry to
your home
Some Nereid coiled in amber foam with curious rock
crystal breasts ?

Or did you treading through the froth call to the brown
    Sidonian
For tidings of Leviathan, Leviathan or Behemoth ?

Or did you when the sun was set climb up the cactus-
    covered slope
To meet your swarthy Ethiop whose body was of pol-
    ished jet ?

Or did you while the earthen skiffs dropped down the
    grey Nilotic flats
At twilight and the flickering bats flew round the tem-
    ple's triple glyphs

Steal to the border of the bar and swim across the silent
    lake
And slink into the vault and make the Pyramid your
    lúpanar

Till from each black sarcophagus rose up the painted
    swathèd dead ?
Or did you lure unto your bed the ivory-horned Trag-
    elaphos ?

Or did you love the god of flies who plagued the Hebrew
    and was splashed
With wine unto the waist ? or Pasht, who had green
    beryls for her eyes ?

Or that young god, the Tyrian, who was more amorous
    than the dove
Of Ashtaroth ? or did you love the god of the Assyrian

Whose wings, like strange transparent talc, rose high
    above his hawk-faced head,
Painted with silver and with red and ribbed with rods of
    Oreichalch ?

Or did huge Apis from his car leap down and lay before
    your feet
Big blossoms of the honey-sweet and honey-coloured
    nenuphar ?

How subtle-secret is your smile ! Did you love none
    then ? Nay, I know
Great Ammon was your bedfellow ! He lay with you
    beside the Nile !

The river-horses in the slime trumpeted when they saw
   him come
Odorous with Syrian galbanum and smeared with
   spikenard and with thyme.

He came along the river bank like some tall galley
   argent-sailed,
He strode across the waters, mailed in beauty, and the
   waters sank.

He strode across the desert sand : he reached the valley
   where you lay :
He waited till the dawn of day : then touched your black
   breasts with his hand.

You kissed his mouth with mouths of flame : you made
   the hornèd god your own :
You stood behind him on his throne : you called him by
   his secret name.

You whispered monstrous oracles into the caverns of his
   ears :
With blood of goats and blood of steers you taught him
   monstrous miracles.

White Ammon was your bedfellow ! Your chamber was
   the steaming Nile !
And with your curved archaic smile you watched his
   passion come and go.

With Syrian oils his brows were bright : and wide-
   spread as a tent at noon
His marble limbs made pale the moon and lent the day
   a larger light.

His long hair was nine cubits' span and coloured like
   that yellow gem
Which hidden in their garment's hem the merchants
   bring from Kurdistan.

His face was as the must that lies upon a vat of new-
   made wine :
The seas could not insapphirine the perfect azure of his
   eyes.

His thick soft throat was white as milk and threaded
   with thin veins of blue :

And curious pearls like frozen dew were broidered on
    his flowing silk.

On pearl and porphyry pedestalled he was too bright to
    look upon :
For on his ivory breast there shone the wondrous ocean-
    emerald,

That mystic moonlit jewel which some diver of the
    Colchian caves
Had found beneath the blackening waves and carried to
    the Colchian witch.

Before his gilded galiot ran naked vine-wreathed cory-
    bants,
And lines of swaying elephants knelt down to draw his
    chariot,

And lines of swarthy Nubians bare up his litter as he
    rode
Down the great granite-paven road between the nod-
    ding peacock fans.

The merchants brought him steatite from Sidon in
    their painted ships :
The meanest cup that touched his lips was fashioned
    from a chrysolite.

The merchants brought him cedar chests of rich ap-
    parel bound with cords ;
His train was borne by Memphian lords : young kings
    were glad to be his guests.

Ten hundred shaven priests did bow to Ammon's altar
    day and night,
Ten hundred lamps did wave their light through Am-
    mon's carven house—and now

Foul snake and speckled adder with their young ones
    crawl from stone to stone
For ruined is the house and prone the great rose-marble
    monolith !

Wild ass or trotting jackal comes and couches in the
    mouldering gates :
Wild satyrs call unto their mates across the fallen fluted
    drums.

And on the summit of the pile the blue-faced ape of
Horus sits
And gibbers while the fig-tree splits the pillars of the
peristyle.

The god is scattered here and there : deep hidden in the
windy sand
I saw his giant granite hand still clenched in impotent
despair.

And many a wandering caravan of stately negroes
silken-shawled,
Crossing the desert halts appalled before the neck that
none can span.

And many a bearded Bedouin draws back his yellow-
striped burnous
To gaze upon the Titan thews of him who was thy
paladin.

Go, seek his fragments on the moor and wash them in
the evening dew,
And from their pieces make anew thy mutilated para-
mour !

Go, seek them where they lie alone and from their
broken pieces make
Thy bruisèd bedfellow ! And wake mad passions in the
senseless stone !

Charm his dull ear with Syrian hymns ! he loved your
body ! oh, be kind,
Pour spikenard on his hair, and wind soft rolls of linen
round his limbs !

Wind round his head the figured coins ! stain with red
fruits those pallid lips !
Weave purple for his shrunken hips ! and purple for his
barren loins !

Away to Egypt ! Have no fear. Only one God has ever
died.
Only one God has let His side be wounded by a soldier's
spear.

But these, thy lovers, are not dead. Still by the
hundred-cubit gate

Dog-faced Anubis sits in state with lotus-lilies for thy
   head.

Still from his chair of porphyry gaunt Memnon strains
   his lidless eyes
Across the empty land, and cries each yellow morning
   unto thee.

And Nilus with his broken horn lies in his black and
   oozy bed
And till thy coming will not spread his waters on the
   withering corn.

Your lovers are not dead, I know. They will rise up and
   hear your voice
And clash their cymbals and rejoice and run to kiss your
   mouth ! And so,

Set wings upon your argosies ! Set horses to your ebon
   car !
Back to your Nile ! Or if you are grown sick of dead
   divinities

Follow some roving lion's spoor across the copper-
   coloured plain,
Reach out and hale him by the mane and bid him be
   your paramour !

Couch by his side upon the grass and set your white
   teeth in his throat
And when you hear his dying note lash your long flanks
   of polished brass

And take a tiger for your mate, whose amber sides are
   flecked with black,
And ride upon his gilded back in triumph through the
   Theban gate,

And toy with him in amorous jests, and when he turns,
   and snarls, and gnaws,
O smite him with your jasper claws ! and bruise him
   with your agate breasts !

Why are you tarrying ? Get hence ! I weary of your
   sullen ways,
I weary of your steadfast gaze, your somnolent magnifi-
   cence.

Your horrible and heavy breath makes the light flicker
    in the lamp,
And on my brow I feel the damp and dreadful dews of
    night and death.

Your eyes are like fantastic moons that shiver in some
    stagnant lake,
Your tongue is like a scarlet snake that dances to fantas-
    tic tunes,

Your pulse makes poisonous melodies, and your black
    throat is like the hole
Left by some torch or burning coal on Saracenic tapes-
    tries.

Away ! The sulphur-coloured stars are hurrying
    through the Western gate !
Away ! Or it may be too late to climb their silent silver
    cars !

See, the dawn shivers round the grey gilt-dialled towers,
    and the rain
Streams down each diamonded pane and blurs with
    tears the wannish day.

What snake-tressed fury fresh from Hell, with uncouth
    gestures and unclean,
Stole from the poppy-drowsy queen and led you to a
    student's cell ?

What songless tongueless ghost of sin crept through the
    curtains of the night,
And saw my taper turning bright, and knocked, and
    bade you enter in ?

Are there not others more accursed, whiter with lepro-
    sies than I ?
Are Abana and Pharphar dry that you come here to
    slake your thirst ?

Get hence, you loathsome mystery ! Hideous animal,
    get hence !
You wake in me each bestial sense, you make me what I
    would not be.

You make my creed a barren sham, you wake foul
    dreams of sensual life,

And Atys with his blood-stained knife were better than
    the thing I am.

False Sphinx! False Sphinx! By reedy Styx old
    Charon, leaning on his oar,
Waits for my coin. Go thou before, and leave me to my
    crucifix,

Whose pallid burden, sick with pain, watches the
    world with wearied eyes,
And weeps for every soul that dies, and weeps for every
    soul in vain.

The Ballad of Reading Gaol

1

He did not wear his scarlet coat,
    For blood and wine are red,
And blood and wine were on his hands
    When they found him with the dead,
The poor dead woman whom he loved,
    And murdered in her bed.

He walked amongst the Trial Men
    In a suit of shabby grey;
A cricket cap was on his head,
    And his step seemed light and gay;
But I never saw a man who looked
    So wistfully at the day.

I never saw a man who looked
    With such a wistful eye
Upon that little tent of blue
    Which prisoners call the sky,
And at every drifting cloud that went
    With sails of silver by.

I walked, with other souls in pain,
    Within another ring,
And was wondering if the man had done
    A great or little thing,
When a voice behind me whispered low,
    " *That fellow's got to swing.*"

Dear Christ ! the very prison walls
   Suddenly seemed to reel,
And the sky above my head became
   Like a casque of scorching steel ;
And, though I was a soul in pain,
   My pain I could not feel.

I only knew what hunted thought
   Quickened his step, and why
He looked upon the garish day
   With such a wistful eye ;
The man had killed the thing he loved,
   And so he had to die.

•

Yet each man kills the thing he loves,
   By each let this be heard,
Some do it with a bitter look,
   Some with a flattering word.
The coward does it with a kiss,
   The brave man with a sword !

Some kill their love when they are young,
   And some when they are old ;
Some strangle with the hands of Lust,
   Some with the hands of Gold :
The kindest use a knife, because
   The dead so soon grow cold.

Some love too little, some too long,
   Some sell, and others buy ;
Some do the deed with many tears,
   And some without a sigh :
For each man kills the thing he loves,
   Yet each man does not die.

He does not die a death of shame
   On a day of dark disgrace,
Nor have a noose about his neck,
   Nor a cloth upon his face,
Nor drop feet foremost through the floor
   Into an empty space.

He does not sit with silent men
   Who watch him night and day ;
Who watch him when he tries to weep,

And when he tries to pray ;
Who watch him lest himself should rob
    The prison of its prey.

He does not wake at dawn to see
    Dread figures throng his room,
The shivering Chaplain robed in white,
    The Sheriff stern with gloom,
And the Governor all in shiny black,
    With the yellow face of Doom.

He does not rise in piteous haste
    To put on convict-clothes,
While some coarse-mouthed Doctor gloats, and notes
    Each new and nerve-twitched pose,
Fingering a watch whose little ticks
    Are like horrible hammer-blows.

He does not feel that sickening thirst
    That sands one's throat, before
The hangman with his gardener's gloves
    Comes through the padded door,
And binds one with three leathern thongs,
    That the throat may thirst no more.

He does not bend his head to hear
    The Burial Office read,
Nor, while the anguish of his soul
    Tells him he is not dead,
Cross his own coffin, as he moves
    Into the hideous shed.

He does not stare upon the air
    Through a little roof of glass :
He does not pray with lips of clay
    For his agony to pass ;
Nor feel upon his shuddering cheek
    The kiss of Caiaphas.

2

Six weeks the guardsman walked the yard,
    In the suit of shabby grey :
His cricket cap was on his head,

And his step seemed light and gay,
But I never saw a man who looked
    So wistfully at the day.

I never saw a man who looked
    With such a wistful eye
Upon that little tent of blue
    Which prisoners call the sky,
And at every wandering cloud that trailed
    Its ravelled fleeces by.

He did not wring his hands, as do
    Those witless men who dare
To try to rear the changeling Hope
    In the cave of black Despair :
He only looked upon the sun,
    And drank the morning air.

He did not wring his hands nor weep,
    Nor did he peek or pine,
But he drank the air as though it held
    Some healthful anodyne ;
With open mouth he drank the sun
    As though it had been wine !

And I and all the souls in pain,
    Who tramped the other ring,
Forgot if we ourselves had done
    A great or little thing,
And watched with gaze of dull amaze
    The man who had to swing.

For strange it was to see him pass
    With a step so light and gay,
And strange it was to see him look
    So wistfully at the day,
And strange it was to think that he
    Had such a debt to pay.

•

For oak and elm have pleasant leaves
    That in the spring-time shoot ;
But grim to see is the gallows-tree,
    With its adder-bitten root,
And, green or dry, a man must die
    Before it bears its fruit !

The loftiest place is that seat of grace
 For which all worldlings try :
But who would stand in hempen band
 Upon a scaffold high,
And through a murderer's collar take
 His last look at the sky ?

It is sweet to dance to violins
 When Love and Life are fair :
To dance to flutes, to dance to lutes
 Is delicate and rare :
But it is not sweet with nimble feet
 To dance upon the air !

So with curious eyes and sick surmise
 We watched him day by day,
And wondered if each one of us
 Would end the self-same way,
For none can tell to what red Hell
 His sightless soul may stray.

At last the dead man walked no more
 Amongst the Trial Men,
And I knew that he was standing up
 In the black dock's dreadful pen,
And that never would I see his face
 For weal or woe again.

Like two doomed ships that pass in storm
 We had crossed each other's way :
But we made no sign, we said no word,
 We had no word to say ;
For we did not meet in the holy night,
 But in the shameful day.

A prison wall was round us both,
 Two outcast men we were :
The world had thrust us from its heart,
 And God from out His care :
And the iron gin that waits for Sin
 Had caught us in its snare.

3

In Debtor's Yard the stones are hard,
    And the dripping wall is high,
So it was there he took the air
    Beneath the leaden sky,
And by each side a Warder walked,
    For fear the man might die.

Or else he sat with those who watched
    His anguish night and day ;
Who watched him when he rose to weep,
    And when he crouched to pray ;
Who watched him lest himself should rob
    Their scaffold of its prey.

The Governor was strong upon
    The Regulations Act :
The Doctor said that Death was but
    A scientific fact :
And twice a day the Chaplain called,
    And left a little tract.

And twice a day he smoked his pipe,
    And drank his quart of beer :
His soul was resolute, and held
    No hiding-place for fear ;
He often said that he was glad
    The hangman's day was near.

But why he said so strange a thing
    No warder dared to ask :
For he to whom a watcher's doom
    Is given as his task,
Must set a lock upon his lips
    And make his face a mask.

Or else he might be moved, and try
    To comfort or console :
And what should Human Pity do
    Pent up in Murderer's Hole ?
What word of grace in such a place
    Could help a brother's soul ?

With slouch and swing around the ring
   We trod the Fools' Parade !
We did not care : we knew we were
   The Devil's Own Brigade :
And shaven head and feet of lead
   Make a merry masquerade.

We tore the tarry rope to shreds
   With blunt and bleeding nails ;
We rubbed the doors, and scrubbed the floors,
   And cleaned the shining rails :
And, rank by rank, we soaped the plank,
   And clattered with the pails.

We sewed the sacks, we broke the stones,
   We turned the dusty drill :
We banged the tins, and bawled the hymns,
   And sweated on the mill :
But in the heart of every man
   Terror was lying still.

So still it lay that every day
   Crawled like a weed-clogged wave :
And we forgot the bitter lot
   That waits for fool and knave,
Till once, as we tramped in from work,
   We passed an open grave.

With yawning mouth the yellow hole
   Gaped for a living thing ;
The very mud cried out for blood
   To the thirsty asphalte ring :
And we knew that ere one dawn grew fair
   Some prisoner had to swing.

Right in we went, with soul intent
   On Death and Dread and Doom :
The hangman, with his little bag,
   Went shuffling through the gloom :
And I trembled as I groped my way
   Into my numbered tomb.

•

That night the empty corridors
   Were full of forms of Fear,

And up and down the iron town
　　Stole feet we could not hear,
And through the bars that hide the stars
　　White faces seemed to peer.

He lay as one who lies and dreams
　　In a pleasant meadow-land,
The watchers watched him as he slept,
　　And could not understand
How one could sleep so sweet a sleep
　　With a hangman close at hand.

But there is no sleep when men must weep
　　Who never yet have wept :
So we—the fool, the fraud, the knave—
　　That endless vigil kept,
And through each brain on hands of pain
　　Another's terror crept.

Alas ! it is a fearful thing
　　To feel another's guilt !
For, right, within, the Sword of Sin
　　Pierced to its poisoned hilt,
And as molten lead were the tears we shed
　　For the blood we had not spilt.

The warders with their shoes of felt
　　Crept by each padlocked door,
And peeped and saw, with eyes of awe,
　　Grey figures on the floor,
And wondered why men knelt to pray
　　Who never prayed before.

All through the night we knelt and prayed,
　　Mad mourners of a corse !
The troubled plumes of midnight shook
　　The plumes upon a hearse :
And bitter wine upon a sponge
　　Was the savour of Remorse.

•

The grey cock crew, the red cock crew,
　　But never came the day :
And crooked shapes of Terror crouched,
　　In the corners where we lay :

And each evil sprite that walks by night
　　Before us seemed to play.

They glided past, they glided fast,
　　Like travellers through a mist :
They mocked the moon in a rigadoon
　　Of delicate turn and twist,
And with formal pace and loathsome grace
　　The phantoms kept their tryst.

With mop and mow, we saw them go,
　　Slim shadows hand in hand :
About, about, in ghostly rout
　　They trod a saraband :
And the damned grotesques made arabesques,
　　Like the wind upon the sand !

With the pirouettes of marionettes,
　　They tripped on pointed tread :
But with flutes of Fear they filled the ear,
　　As their grisly masque they led,
And loud they sang, and long they sang,
　　For they sang to wake the dead.

" Oho ! " they cried, " *The world is wide,*
　　But fettered limbs go lame !
And once, or twice, to throw the dice
　　Is a gentlemanly game,
But he does not win who plays with Sin
　　In the secret House of Shame."

No things of air these antics were,
　　That frolicked with such glee :
To men whose lives were held in gyves,
　　And whose feet might not go free,
Ah ! wounds of Christ ! they were living things
　　Most terrible to see.

Around, around, they waltzed and wound ;
　　Some wheeled in smirking pairs ;
With the mincing step of a demirep
　　Some sidled up the stairs :
And with subtle sneer, and fawning leer,
　　Each helped us at our prayers.

The morning wind began to moan,
　　But still the night went on :

Through its giant loom the web of gloom
  Crept till each thread was spun :
And, as we prayed, we grew afraid
  Of the Justice of the Sun.

The moaning wind went wandering round
  The weeping prison-wall :
Till like a wheel of turning steel
  We felt the minutes crawl :
O moaning wind ! what had we done
  To have such a seneschal ?

At last I saw the shadowed bars,
  Like a lattice wrought in lead,
Move right across the whitewashed wall
  That faced my three-plank bed,
And I knew that somewhere in the world
  God's dreadful dawn was red.

At six o'clock we cleaned our cells,
  At seven all was still,
But the sough and swing of a mighty wing
  The prison seemed to fill,
For the Lord of Death with icy breath
  Had entered in to kill.

He did not pass in purple pomp,
  Nor ride a moon-white steed.
Three yards of cord and a sliding board
  Are all the gallows' need :
So with rope of shame the Herald came
  To do the secret deed.

We were as men who through a fen
  Of filthy darkness grope :
We did not dare to breathe a prayer,
  Or to give our anguish scope :
Something was dead in each of us,
  And what was dead was Hope.

For Man's grim Justice goes its way,
  And will not swerve aside :
It slays the weak, it slays the strong,
  It has a deadly stride :
With iron heel it slays the strong,
  The monstrous parricide !

We waited for the stroke of eight :
    Each tongue was thick with thirst :
For the stroke of eight is the stroke of Fate
    That makes a man accursed,
And Fate will use a running noose
    For the best man and the worst.

We had no other thing to do,
    Save to wait for the sign to come :
So, like things of stone in a valley lone,
    Quiet we sat and dumb :
But each man's heart beat thick and quick,
    Like a madman on a drum !

With sudden shock the prison-clock
    Smote on the shivering air,
And from all the gaol rose up a wail
    Of impotent despair,
Like the sound that frightened marshes hear
    From some leper in his lair.

And as one sees most fearful things
    In the crystal of a dream,
We saw the greasy hempen rope
    Hooked to the blackened beam,
And heard the prayer the hangman's snare
    Strangled into a scream.

And all the woe that moved him so
    That he gave that bitter cry,
And the wild regrets, and the bloody sweats,
    None knew so well as I :
For he who lives more lives than one
    More deaths than one must die.

4

There is no chapel on the day
    On which they hang a man :
The Chaplain's heart is far too sick,
    Or his face is far too wan,
Or there is that written in his eyes
    Which none should look upon.

So they kept us close till nigh on noon,
  And then they rang the bell,
And the warders with their jingling keys
  Opened each listening cell,
And down the iron stair we tramped,
  Each from his separate Hell.

Out into God's sweet air we went,
  But not in wonted way,
For this man's face was white with fear,
  And that man's face was grey,
And I never saw sad men who looked
  So wistfully at the day.

I never saw sad men who looked
  With such a wistful eye
Upon that little tent of blue
  We prisoners called the sky,
And at every happy cloud that passed
  In such strange freedom by.

But there were those amongst us all
  Who walked with downcast head,
And knew that, had each got his due,
  They should have died instead :
He had but killed a thing that lived,
  Whilst they had killed the dead.

For he who sins a second time
  Wakes a dead soul to pain,
And draws it from its spotted shroud,
  And makes it bleed again,
And makes it bleed great gouts of blood,
  And makes it bleed in vain !

·

Like ape or clown, in monstrous garb
  With crooked arrows starred,
Silently we went round and round
  The slippery asphalte yard ;
Silently we went round and round,
  And no man spoke a word.

Silently we went round and round,
  And through each hollow mind

The Memory of dreadful things
    Rushed like a dreadful wind,
And Horror stalked before each man,
    And Terror crept behind.

·

The warders strutted up and down,
    And watched their herd of brutes,
Their uniforms were spick and span,
    And they wore their Sunday suits.
But we knew the work they had been at,
    By the quicklime on their boots.

For where a grave had opened wide,
    There was no grave at all :
Only a stretch of mud and sand
    By the hideous prison-wall,
And a little heap of burning lime,
    That the man should have his pall.

For he has a pall, this wretched man,
    Such as few men can claim :
Deep down below a prison-yard,
    Naked for greater shame,
He lies, with fetters on each foot,
    Wrapt in a sheet of flame !

And all the while the burning lime
    Eats flesh and bone away,
It eats the brittle bone by night,
    And the soft flesh by day,
It eats the flesh and bone by turns,
    But it eats the heart alway.

·

For three long years they will not sow
    Or root or seedling there :
For three long years the unblessed spot
    Will sterile be and bare,
And look upon the wondering sky
    With unreproachful stare.

They think a murderer's heart would taint
    Each simple seed they sow.

It is not true ! God's kindly earth
Is kindlier than men know,
And the red rose would but blow more red,
The white rose whiter blow.

Out of his mouth a red, red rose !
Out of his heart a white !
For who can say by what strange way
Christ brings His will to light,
Since the barren staff the pilgrim bore
Bloomed in the great Pope's sight ?

But neither milk-white rose nor red
May bloom in prison-air ;
The shard, the pebble, and the flint,
Are what they give us there :
For flowers have been known to heal
A common man's despair.

So never will wine-red rose or white,
Petal by petal, fall
On that stretch of mud and sand that lies
By the hideous prison-wall,
To tell the men who tramp the yard
That God's Son died for all.

Yet though the hideous prison-wall
Still hems him round and round,
And a spirit may not walk by night
That is with fetters bound,
And a spirit may but weep that lies
In such unholy ground,

He is at peace—this wretched man—
At peace, or will be soon :
There is no thing to make him mad,
Nor does Terror walk at noon,
For the lampless Earth in which he lies
Has neither Sun nor Moon.

They hanged him as a beast is hanged !
They did not even toll
A requiem that might have brought
Rest to his startled soul,

But hurriedly they took him out,
    And hid him in a hole.

The warders stripped him of his clothes,
    And gave him to the flies :
They mocked the swollen purple throat,
    And the stark and staring eyes :
And with laughter loud they heaped the shroud
    In which the convict lies.

The Chaplain would not kneel to pray
    By his dishonoured grave :
Nor mark it with that blessed Cross
    That Christ for sinners gave,
Because the man was one of those
    Whom Christ came down to save.

Yet all is well ; he has but passed
    To Life's appointed bourne :
And alien tears will fill for him
    Pity's long-broken urn,
For his mourners will be outcast men,
    And outcasts always mourn.

5

I know not whether Laws be right,
    Or whether Laws be wrong ;
All that we know who lie in gaol
    Is that the wall is strong ;
And that each day is like a year,
    A year whose days are long.

But this I know, that every Law
    That men hath made for Man,
Since first Man took his brother's life,
    And the sad world began,
But straws the wheat and saves the chaff
    With a most evil fan.

This too I know—and wise it were
    If each could know the same—
That every prison that men build
    Is built with bricks of shame,

And bound with bars lest Christ should see
    How men their brothers maim.

With bars they blur the gracious moon,
    And blind the goodly sun ;
And they do well to hide their Hell,
    For in it things are done
That Son of God nor son of Man
    Ever should look upon !

•

The vilest deeds like poison weeds,
    Bloom well in prison-air ;
It is only what is good in Man
    That wastes and withers there :
Pale Anguish keeps the heavy gate,
    And the Warder is Despair.

For they starve the little frightened child
    Till it weeps both night and day :
And they scourge the weak, and flog the fool,
    And gibe the old and grey,
And some grow mad, and all grow bad,
    And none a word may say.

Each narrow cell in which we dwell
    Is a foul and dark latrine,
And the fetid breath of living Death
    Chokes up each grated screen,
And all, but Lust, is turned to dust
    In Humanity's machine.

The brackish water that we drink
    Creeps with a loathsome slime,
And the bitter bread they weigh in scales
    Is full of chalk and lime,
And Sleep will not lie down, but walks
    Wild-eyed, and cries to Time.

•

But though lean Hunger and green Thirst
    Like asp with adder fight,
We have little care of prison fare,

For what chills and kills outright
Is that every stone one lifts by day
    Becomes one's heart by night.

With midnight always in one's heart,
    And twilight in one's cell,
We turn the crank, or tear the rope,
    Each in his separate Hell,
And the silence is more awful far
    Than the sound of a brazen bell.

And never a human voice comes near
    To speak a gentle word :
And the eye that watches through the door
    Is pitiless and hard :
And by all forgot, we rot and rot,
    With soul and body marred.

And thus we rust Life's iron chain,
    Degraded and alone :
And some men curse, and some men weep,
    And some men make no moan :
But God's eternal Laws are kind
    And break the heart of stone.

And every human heart that breaks,
    In prison-cell or yard,
Is as that broken box that gave
    Its treasure to the Lord,
And filled the unclean leper's house
    With the scent of costliest nard.

Ah ! happy they whose hearts can break
    And peace of pardon win !
How else may man make straight his plan
    And cleanse his soul from Sin ?
How else but through a broken heart
    May Lord Christ enter in ?

•

And he of the swollen purple throat,
    And the stark and staring eyes,
Waits for the holy hands that took
    The Thief to Paradise ;

And a broken and a contrite heart
  The Lord will not despise.

The man in red who reads the Law
  Gave him three weeks of life,
Three little weeks in which to heal
  His soul of his soul's strife,
And cleanse from every blot of blood
  The hand that held the knife.

And with tears of blood he cleansed the hand,
  The hand that held the steel :
For only blood can wipe out blood,
  And only tears can heal :
And the crimson stain that was of Cain
  Became Christ's snow-white seal.

6

In Reading gaol by Reading town
  There is a pit of shame,
And in it lies a wretched man
  Eaten by teeth of flame,
In a burning winding-sheet he lies,
  And his grave has got no name.

And there, till Christ call forth the dead,
  In silence let him lie :
No need to waste the foolish tear,
  Or heave the windy sigh :
The man had killed the thing he loved,
  And so he had to die.

And all men kill the thing they love,
  By all let this be heard,
Some do it with a bitter look,
  Some with a flattering word,
The coward does it with a kiss,
  The brave man with a sword !

The Harlot's House

We caught the tread of dancing feet,
We loitered down the moonlit street,
And stopped beneath the harlot's house.

Inside, above the din and fray,
We heard the loud musicians play
The " Treues Liebes Herz " of Strauss.

Like strange mechanical grotesques,
Making fantastic arabesques,
The shadows raced across the blind.

We watched the ghostly dancers spin
To sound of horn and violin,
Like black leaves wheeling in the wind.

Like wire-pulled automatons,
Slim silhouetted skeletons
Went sidling through the slow quadrille.

They took each other by the hand,
And danced a stately saraband ;
Their laughter echoed thin and shrill.

Sometimes a clockwork puppet pressed
A phantom lover to her breast,
Sometimes they seemed to try to sing.

Sometimes a horrible marionette
Came out, and smoked its cigarette
Upon the steps like a live thing.

Then, turning to my love, I said,
" The dead are dancing with the dead,
The dust is whirling with the dust."

But she—she heard the violin,
And left my side, and entered in :
Love passed into the house of lust.

Then suddenly the tune went false,
The dancers wearied of the waltz,
The shadows ceased to wheel and whirl.

And down the long and silent street,
The dawn, with silver-sandalled feet,
Crept like a frightened girl.

Fantaisies Décoratives

Le Panneau*

Under the rose-tree's dancing shade
    There stands a little ivory girl,
    Pulling the leaves of pink and pearl
With pale green nails of polished jade.

The red leaves fall upon the mould,
    The white leaves flutter, one by one,
    Down to a blue bowl where the sun,
Like a great dragon, writhes in gold.

The white leaves float upon the air,
    The red leaves flutter idly down,
    Some fall upon her yellow gown,
And some upon her raven hair.

She takes an amber lute and sings,
    And as she sings a silver crane
    Begins his scarlet neck to strain,
And flap his burnished metal wings.

She takes a lute of amber bright,
    And from the thicket where he lies
    Her lover, with his almond eyes,
Watches her movements in delight.

And now she gives a cry of fear,
    And tiny tears begin to start ;
    A thorn has wounded with its dart
The pink-veined sea-shell of her ear.

And now she laughs a merry note :
    There has fallen a petal of the rose

* The Panel.

Just where the yellow satin shows
The blue-veined flower of her throat.

With pale green nails of polished jade,
  Pulling the leaves of pink and pearl,
  There stands a little ivory girl
Under the rose-tree's dancing shade.

Les Ballons

Against these turbid turquoise skies
  The light and luminous balloons
  Dip and drift like satin moons,
Drift like silken butterflies ;

Reel with every windy gust,
  Rise and reel like dancing girls,
  Float like strange transparent pearls,
Fall and float like silver dust.

Now to the low leaves they cling,
  Each with coy fantastic pose,
  Each a petal of a rose
Straining at a gossamer string.

Then to the tall trees they climb,
  Like thin globes of amethyst,
  Wandering opals keeping tryst
With the rubies of the lime.

Canzonet

  I have no store
Of gryphon-guarded gold ;
  Now, as before,
Bare is the shepherd's fold.
  Rubies nor pearls
Have I to gem thy throat ;
  Yet woodland girls
Have loved the shepherd's note.

Then pluck a reed
And bid me sing to thee,
  For I would feed
Thine ears with melody,
  Who art more fair
Than fairest fleur-de-lys,
  More sweet and rare
Than sweetest ambergris.

What dost thou fear ?
Young Hyacinth is slain,
  Pan is not here,
And will not come again.
  No horned Faun
Treads down the yellow leas,
  No God at dawn
Steals through the olive trees.

Hylas is dead,
Nor will he e'er divine
  Those little red
Rose-petalled lips of thine.
  On the high hill
No ivory dryads play,
  Silver and still
Sinks the sad autumn day.

Symphony in Yellow

An omnibus across the bridge
  Crawls like a yellow butterfly,
  And, here and there, a passer-by
Shows like a little restless midge.

Big barges full of yellow hay
  Are moved against the shadowy wharf,
  And, like a yellow silken scarf,
The thick fog hangs along the quay.

The yellow leaves begin to fade
  And flutter from the Temple elms,
  And at my feet the pale green Thames
Lies like a rod of rippled jade.

In the Forest

Out of the mid-wood's twilight
  Into the meadow's dawn,
Ivory limbed and brown eyed,
  Flashes my Faun !

He skips through the copses singing,
  And his shadow dances along,
And I know not which I should follow,
  Shadow or song !

O Hunter, snare me his shadow !
  O Nightingale, catch me his strain !
Else moonstruck with music and madness
  I track him in vain !

To L. L.

Could we dig up this long-buried treasure,
  Were it worth the pleasure,
We never could learn love's song,
  We are parted too long.

Could the passionate past that is fled
  Call back its dead,
Could we live it all over again,
  Were it worth the pain !

I remember we used to meet
  By an ivied seat,
And you warbled each pretty word
  With the air of a bird ;

And your voice had a quaver in it,
  Just like a linnet,
And shook, as the blackbird's throat
  With its last big note ;

And your eyes, they were green and grey
  Like an April day,

But lit into amethyst
    When I stooped and kissed ;

And your mouth, it would never smile
    For a long, long while,
Then it rippled all over with laughter
    Five minutes after.

You were always afraid of a shower,
    Just like a flower :
I remember you started and ran
    When the rain began.

I remember I never could catch you,
    For no one could match you,
You had wonderful, luminous, fleet
    Little wings to your feet.

I remember your hair—did I tie it ?
    For it always ran riot—
Like a tangled sunbeam of gold :
    These things are old.

I remember so well the room,
    And the lilac bloom
That beat at the dripping pane
'   In the warm June rain ;

And the colour of your gown,
    It was amber-brown,
And two yellow satin bows
    From your shoulders rose.

And the handkerchief of French lace
    Which you held to your face—
Had a small tear left a stain ?
    Or was it the rain ?

On your hand as it waved adieu
    There were veins of blue ;
In your voice as it said good-bye
    Was a petulant cry,

" You have only wasted your life."
    (Ah, that was the knife !)
When I rushed through the garden gate
    It was all too late.

Could we live it over again,
　Were it worth the pain,
Could the passionate past that is fled
　Call back its dead !

Well, if my heart must break,
　Dear love, for your sake,
It will break in music, I know,
　Poets' hearts break so.

But strange that I was not told
　That the brain can hold
In a tiny ivory cell,
　God's heaven and hell.

Alphabetical List of Titles

Alphabetical List of First Lines